Hello, Beautiful!

Furry Animals

WORLD BOOK

www.worldbook.com

World Book, Inc.
180 North LaSalle Street, Suite 900
Chicago, Illinois 60601
USA

For information about other World Book publications, visit our website at www.worldbook.com or call 1-800-WORLDBK (967-5325).

For information about sales to schools and libraries, call 1-800-975-3250 (United States), or 1-800-837-5365 (Canada).

Library of Congress Cataloging-in-Publication Data for this volume has been applied for.

Hello, Beautiful!
ISBN: 978-0-7166-3567-3 (set, hc.)

Furry Animals
ISBN: 978-0-7166-3573-4 (hc.)

Also available as:
ISBN: 978-0-7166-3583-3 (e-book)

Printed in China by Shenzhen Wing King Tong Paper Products Co., Ltd., Shenzhen, Guangdong
1st printing July 2018

Photographic credits:

Cover: © Shutterstock.

© iStockphoto 24-25; © Shutterstock 4, 7-23, 26-29.

Staff

Writer: Grace Guibert

Executive Committee

President
Jim O'Rourke

Vice President and
Editor in Chief
Paul A. Kobasa

Vice President, Finance
Donald D. Keller

Vice President, Marketing
Jean Lin

Vice President,
International Sales
Maksim Rutenberg

Vice President, Technology
Jason Dole

Director, Human Resources
Bev Ecker

Editorial

Director, New Print
Tom Evans

Managing Editor, New Print
Jeff De La Rosa

Senior Editor, New Print
Shawn Brennan

Editor, New Print
Grace Guibert

Librarian
S. Thomas Richardson

Manager, Contracts &
Compliance (Rights &
Permissions)
Loranne K. Shields

Manager, Indexing Services
David Pofelski

Digital

Director, Digital Content
Development
Emily Kline

Director, Digital Product
Development
Erika Meller

Manager, Digital Products
Jonathan Wills

Graphics and Design

Senior Art Director
Tom Evans

Senior Visual
Communications Designer
Melanie Bender

Media Researcher
Rosalia Bledsoe

Manufacturing/
Production

Manufacturing Manager
Anne Fritzinger

Proofreader
Nathalie Strassheim

Contents

Introduction

Welcome to "Hello, Beautiful!" picture books!

This book is about furry animals from around the globe. Each book in the "Hello, Beautiful!" series uses large, colorful photographs and a few words to describe our world to children who are not yet reading on their own or are beginning to learn to read. For the benefit of both grown-up and child readers, a picture key is included in the back of the volume to describe each photograph and specific type of animal in more detail.

"Hello, Beautiful!" books can help pre-readers and starting readers get into the habit of having fun with books and learning from them, too. With pre-readers, a grown-up reader (parent, grandparent, librarian, teacher, older brother or sister) can point to the words on each page as he or she speaks them aloud to help the listening child associate the concept of text with the object or idea it describes.

Large, colorful photographs give pre-readers plenty to see while they listen to the reader. If no reader is available, pre-readers can "read" on their own, turning the pages of the book and speaking their own stories about what they see. For new readers, the photographs provide visual hints about the words on the page. Often, these words describe the specific type of animal shown. This animal may not be representative of all species, or types, of that animal.

This book displays some furry animals that hop, crawl, climb, or swim all over the world! Some of these animals are becoming extinct as they lose their habitats. Help inspire respect and care for these important and beautiful animals by sharing this "Hello, Beautiful!" book with a child soon.

Hello, beautiful bear!

You are a **brown** bear. You sleep through the cold winter in your den. Your thick, soft fur helps keep you warm.

You catch and eat lots of fish in summertime!

Chinchilla

Hello, beautiful chinchilla!

You are a long-tailed chinchilla. We love your thick, shiny, blue-gray fur.

You only come out at night—to look for food!

Dog

Hello, beautiful dog!

You are a puli. You have woolly hair. It looks like small ropes!

You are a great watchdog. You like to run and play!

Fox

Hello, beautiful fox!

You are an Arctic fox. You live where it is very cold. Your thick, white fur keeps you warm.

You are the same color as the snow. Other animals cannot see you!

Kangaroo

Hello, beautiful kangaroo!

You are a **red** kangaroo. Thick fur covers your body.

You are a great hopper!

Your baby
stays safe in
a pouch on
your belly!

Lemur

Hello, beautiful lemur!

You are a ring-tailed lemur. You look like a furry monkey!

You have a striped tail. You mainly live on the ground.

Lion

Hello, beautiful lion!

You are a male African lion.
You have long, thick hair
around your head and neck.

You hunt other animals to
eat. The color of your fur
helps you hide in the grass.

Hello, beautiful mouse!

You are a house mouse.
You have **grayish-brown** fur,
round ears, a long tail,
and whiskers.

You look for food in our house!

Musk ox

Hello, beautiful musk ox!

Your long, shaggy hair keeps you warm.

You live in a big group with your oxen family and friends. This helps keep you safe!

Otter

Hello, beautiful otter!

You are a sea otter. You love to float on the water on your back.

Your thick, **brown** fur keeps your skin warm and dry.

Panda

Hello, beautiful panda!

You are a giant panda. You have **black** and white fur.

You love to eat a plant called bamboo. You eat a lot of it every day!

Sloth

Hello, beautiful sloth!

You are a three-toed sloth. You climb s-l-o-w-l-y through trees. You like to hang upside down! Your fur makes you hard to see in the branches.

Picture Key

Learn more about these furry animals! Use the picture keys below to learn where each animal lives, how big it grows, and its favorite foods!

Bear

Hello, beautiful bear!

You are a **brown** bear. You sleep through the cold winter in your den. Your thick, soft fur helps keep you warm.

You catch and eat lots of fish in summertime!

Chinchilla

Hello, beautiful chinchilla!

You are a long-tailed chinchilla. We love your thick, shiny, **blue-gray** fur.

You only come out at night—to look for food!

Dog

Hello, beautiful dog!

You are a puli. You have woolly hair. It looks like small ropes!

You are a great watchdog. You like to run and play!

Pages 6-7 Bear
Brown bears live in Asia, Europe, and North America. They vary widely in size depending on the region. Brown bears may average from 100 to 1,500 pounds (45 to 680 kilograms). They have an extremely broad diet that can include berries, grass, fruits, nuts, mammals, reptiles, fish, and honey.

Pages 8-9 Chinchilla
Long-tailed chinchillas *(chihn CHIHL uhz)* are native to the Andes Mountains in northern Chile. They are about 12 inches (30 centimeters) in length, with a tail measuring up to $^1/_3$ the length of the body. In the wild, chinchillas eat grasses, bulbs, and roots. Pet chinchillas should be fed scientifically prepared pellets, as well as grains, fruits, vegetables, and hay.

Pages 10-11 Dog
The puli *(POO lee)* originated in the central European country of Hungary. This breed of dog stands about 17 inches (43 centimeters) tall at the shoulder. Owners should feed the puli dog food appropriate for medium-sized dogs to ensure they receive the proper nutrients. Pulis are energetic dogs that need exercise.

Fox

Hello, beautiful fox!

You are an Arctic fox. You live where it is very cold. Your thick, **white** fur keeps you warm.

You are the same color as the snow. Other animals cannot see you!

Kangaroo

Hello, beautiful kangaroo!

You are a **red** kangaroo. Thick fur covers your body.

You are a great hopper!

Your baby stays safe in a pouch on your belly!

Lemur

Hello, beautiful lemur!

You are a ring-tailed lemur. You look like a furry monkey!

You have a **striped** tail. You mainly live on the ground.

Pages 12-13 Fox
The Arctic fox lives on the treeless coastal areas and islands of the Arctic Ocean. It grows about 20 inches (50 centimeters) long, not including its tail, and weighs from 2 to 20 pounds (1 to 9 kilograms). Arctic foxes feed on birds, birds' eggs, and small mammals. When food is scarce, these foxes will travel long distances to feed on animal remains left behind by other animals.

Pages 14-15 Kangaroo
The red kangaroo *(KANG guh ROO)* is native to the deserts and dry grasslands of central Australia. Adult males may weigh as much as 187 pounds (85 kilograms) and stand up to 6 feet (1.8 meters) tall. Most red kangaroos weigh about 110 pounds (50 kilograms) and reach about 5 feet (1.5 meters) in height. They feed on grasses and shrubs. They get plenty of water from these plants, so they can survive when their water supply is limited.

Pages 16-17 Lemur
Ring-tailed lemurs *(LEE muhrz)* live on the southwest part of the African island country of Madagascar. Unlike other lemurs, the ring-tailed variety usually dwells on the ground rather than in trees. Ring-tailed lemurs grow to be about 15 inches (38 centimeters) long. Lemurs eat fruit and leaves. They also eat birds and their eggs, and insects and other small animals.

Pages 18-19 Lion

Lion

Hello, beautiful lion!

You are a male African lion. You have long, thick hair around your head and neck.

You hunt other animals to eat. The color of your fur helps you hide in the grass.

African lions live in the eastern part of central Africa and in southern Africa, primarily within protected reserves. Males usually weigh from 350 to 400 pounds (159 to 180 kilograms). Females are smaller. Lions prey on large animals like zebra, antelope, buffalo, and warthogs. But they will also eat fish, turtles, guineafowl, and other animals they can catch.

Pages 20-21 Mouse

Mouse

Hello, beautiful mouse!

You are a house mouse. You have grayish-brown fur, round ears, a long tail, and whiskers.

You look for food in our house!

The house mouse originated in Asia, then spread through Europe and the rest of the world. House mice are usually from 2 1/2 to 3 1/2 inches (6 to 9 centimeters) long without the tail and weigh 1/2 to 1 ounce (14 to 28 grams). Outdoor house mice eat seeds, insects, and plants. Indoor house mice eat bread, cereal, crackers, pet food, and other household food.

Pages 22-23 Musk ox

Musk ox

Hello, beautiful musk ox!

Your long, shaggy hair keeps you warm.

You live in a big group with your oxen family and friends. This helps keep you safe!

Musk oxen live in the cold Arctic plains. *Bulls* (males) measure about 4 to 5 feet (1.2 to 1.5 meters) tall at the shoulder and weigh about 750 pounds (340 kilograms). *Cows* (females) are smaller. Musk oxen eat grass, mosses, and other tundra plants, roots, and lichens.

Pages 24-25 Otter

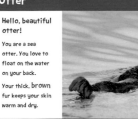

Otter

Hello, beautiful otter!

You are a sea otter. You love to float on the water on your back.

Your thick, brown fur keeps your skin warm and dry.

Sea otters live in the North Pacific Ocean, largely concentrated near the shores of North America and Siberia. Most sea otters grow from 4 to 5 feet (1.2 to 1.5 meters) long and weigh from 60 to 85 pounds (27 to 39 kilograms). A large male, however, may weigh up to 100 pounds (45 kilograms). Sea otters feed on abalones, clams, crabs, fish, mussels, octopuses, sea urchins, and squids.

Pages 26-27 Panda

Panda

Hello, beautiful panda!

You are a giant panda. You have black and white fur.

You love to eat a plant called bamboo. You eat a lot of it every day!

The giant panda lives in the bamboo forests on upper mountain slopes of central China. It grows to about 5 to 6 feet (1.5 to 1.8 meters) long. Adults weigh about 200 to 300 pounds (90 to 140 kilograms). Giant pandas eat bamboo shoots, stems, and leaves— as much as 85 pounds (39 kilograms) daily.

Pages 28-29 Sloth

Sloth

Hello, beautiful sloth!

You are a three-toed sloth. You climb s-l-o-w-l-y through trees. You like to hang upside down! Your fur makes you hard to see in the branches.

Three-toed sloths live in the rain forests of Central and South America. They measure 15 to 30 inches (38 to 76 centimeters) long and weigh 5 to 23 pounds (2.3 to 10.5 kilograms). Three-toed sloths feed mostly on leaves. During the rainy season, their fur may turn green from the algae that grows in it.

Index